P9-BJR-134

# WORLD CULTURES

# Living in the
# Arctic

Neil Morris

Chicago, Illinois

© 2008 Raintree
Published by Raintree,
a division of Reed Elsevier Inc.
Chicago, Illinois

Customer Service  888–454–2279

Visit our website at www.heinemannraintree.com

All rights reserved. No part of this publication may be reproduced or transmitted in any form or by any means, electronic or mechanical, including photocopying, recording, taping, or any information storage and retrieval system, without permission in writing from the publisher.

Designed by Richard Parker and Manhattan Design
Printed and bound in China by CTPS

12 11 10
10 9 8 7 6 5 4 3 2

**Library of Congress Cataloging-in-Publication Data**
Morris, Neil, 1946-
Living in the Arctic.
p. cm. -- (World cultures)
Includes bibliographical references and index.
ISBN-13: 978-1-4109-2815-3 (library binding–hardcover)
ISBN-10: 1-4109-2815-2 (library binding–hardcover)
ISBN-13: 978-1-4109-2824-5 (pbk.)
ISBN-10: 1-4109-2824-1 (pbk.)
1. Inuit--Social life and customs--Juvenile literature.
2. Arctic regions--Social life and customs--Juvenile literature. I. Title.
E99.E7M8412 2007
971.9004'9712--dc22

                    2007003279

**Acknowledgments**
The publishers would like to thank the following for permission to reproduce photographs: Accent Alaska p. **21**; Alamy Images/ Bryan and Cherry Alexander pp. **18, 23, 25**; Bryan and Cherry Alexander pp. **5, 6, 11, 13, 16, 19, 22, 24, 29**; Art Directors and Trip/ Norman Price pp. **9, 12, 26**; Corbis pp. **14** (Catherine Karnow), **15** (Staffan Widstrand), **28** (Krause, Johansen/ Archivo Icongraficao, SA); Eye Ubiquitous/ Hutchison p. **17**; Getty Images pp. **10** (Taxi), **20** (Stone); Harcourt Education Ltd/ Tudor Photography p. **27** (all); Photographers Direct/ Wilderness Photographic Library p. **8**; Topham Picturepoint/ The Image Works p. **7**.

Illustrations by International Mapping.

Cover photograph of an Inuit hunter and his dogsled team crossing the frozen sea of Baffin Bay, reproduced with permission of Corbis/ Layne Kennedy.

Every effort has been made to contact copyright holders of any material reproduced in this book. Any omissions will be rectified in subsequent printings if notice is given to the publishers.

# Contents

Some words are printed in bold, **like this**. You can find out what they mean on page 31.

# People of the Far North

The Inuit are people who live in the **Arctic**. The Arctic is a very cold area at the top of the world, around the North Pole. Inuit live in Canada, Greenland, Alaska, and Russia. "Inuit" means "people" in Inuktitut. Inuktitut is the Inuit language. You may have heard the Inuit called Eskimos. This name probably came from Native American words. Today, they prefer to be called Inuit.

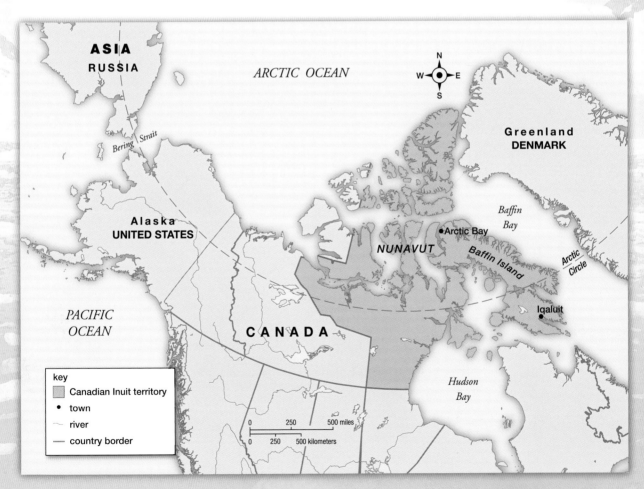

▲ The Inuit live in the Arctic. The Canadian Inuit live in Nunavut.

# OUR LAND

Canada is a country in North America. In 1999 the Inuit people of Canada gained control over their homeland. This **territory** is called Nunavut (see map opposite). The territory covers much of northeastern Canada. "Nunavut" means "our land" in the Inuit language. Today, about 23,000 Inuit live in Nunavut.

▲ Young Inuit get used to long, cold winters. They also live with short, cool summers.

## Snow and ice

Snow and ice cover the ground for most of the year in the Arctic. The landscape is called **tundra**. Trees cannot grow there. The tundra does have low **shrubs**. There are also **mosses** and other small plants. Some plants cover the ground with flowers in summer. Some produce berries.

**5**

# Inuit Communities

Most Inuit live in a **settlement**. Settlements are places where people live. About one thousand people live in each settlement. They have schools and some stores. There is usually a radio station. This tells people local news and weather reports. People keep in touch by phone and radio. Today, they also use the Internet.

▲ This small settlement curves around an icy bay.

## Place of many fish

The capital of Nunavut **territory** is Iqaluit. "Iqaluit" means "place of many fish." It is on the Baffin Island coast (see map on page 4). Inuit hunters used to camp here. It was a good place to fish. Today, more than 6,000 people live in the town. It is the largest Inuit **community**. It even has an airport.

▲ Fishermen catch fish, such as Arctic char, in the waters near Iqaluit.

## MOVING AROUND

The Inuit did not always live in settlements. Traditionally, they moved around in small groups. They hunted and fished as they went. They built camps to rest in at night and stayed there for several days or weeks.

# At Home

Many Inuit houses are wooden. There are no trees in the **Arctic**. The wooden houses are made in sections. They are brought to the **communities** by ship. In many houses, children live with their parents, grandparents, and even great-grandparents.

▲ Today, Inuit houses are built on stilts. This raises them off the frozen, uneven ground.

## Snow houses

Inuit hunters make snow houses to shelter them from the wind and cold. We often call these dome-shaped shelters igloos. Hunters teach children how to cut blocks of hard snow. They learn how to fit the blocks together to make a house. This will help them survive if they are caught in a freezing storm.

▸ A snow house is called an *igluvigaq* in the Inuit language. Children often learn to build them at Inuit festivals. They also learn this skill in survival classes.

## SEASONAL SHELTERS

Years ago, Inuit families lived in two other kinds of houses. They built a house for the winter. They piled up stones, washed-up **driftwood**, and whalebone. The walls and roof were covered with **moss** and grass. This winter home was called a sod house. In summer, families lived in tents. The tents were made of sealskin.

# Keeping Warm

The Inuit have always worn clothes made of animal skins. Today, many young Inuit wear modern versions of traditional clothing. These are made of wool, cotton, nylon, or an artificial fleece. They are usually still trimmed with fur. The best way to keep warm is to trap a layer of air near the body. This means loose-fitting clothes are best.

▲ Inuit mittens and boots are made of sealskin. Fur-trimmed hoods keep out the cold.

# BABY CARRIER

Inuit mothers wear a special jacket. It is called an *amauti*. It is really useful because it is also a baby carrier. The mother carries her child close to her body. This keeps the baby warm in the coldest weather.

▸ This mother is carrying her baby in the large hood of her *amauti* jacket.

## Parka

The favorite jacket for **Arctic** conditions is called a parka. It is hooded and windproof. It used to be made of **caribou** (similar to reindeer) skin. The hairs of caribou fur trap in extra air. This makes the jacket very warm. Today, many parkas are made from modern materials such as nylon. The Inuit wear the parkas inside out, so that the warm fur is next to their skin.

# At School

Most Inuit elementary school children are taught in the Inuit language, Inuktitut. In high school, classes are usually in English. Inuit children learn all the basic subjects, such as math, science, and geography. Schools in many areas also teach traditional **Arctic** skills.

◄ The language of Inuktitut has many symbols. Children learn how to read and write the symbols.

◀ A stop sign in Iqaluit, the capital of Nanavut, is written in both English and Inuktitut.

## Inuit language

Inuktitut is an official language in the Nunavut **territory** of Canada. English and French are also spoken. Inuktitut has many different **dialects**. This means the language can vary between regions. Inuktitut is written as a set of symbols. These symbols or characters build up words. The words can also be written in the English alphabet. For example, "polar bear" is *nanuk*, "bear cub" is *nanertak*, and "bearskin" is *nanurark*.

## TRADITIONAL SKILLS

Many Arctic schools teach traditional skills as well as modern subjects. School children learn about their Inuit history and customs, including their arts, crafts, and music. Older children learn how to live and survive in the harsh Arctic climate.

13

# Food

Meat and fish have always been a large part of the Inuit diet. People eat **caribou**, seal, and whale meat. Few fruits and vegetables grow in the cold climate. There are some **Arctic** berries, such as cranberries and blackberries. Vegetables have to be shipped or flown in. This makes them expensive.

▲ A hunter dries arctic char, so that it can be eaten later. Dried fish is a delicacy (special food) for the Inuit.

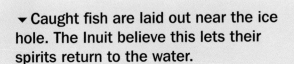
▼ Caught fish are laid out near the ice hole. The Inuit believe this lets their spirits return to the water.

## THROUGH THE ICE

The Inuit still use a traditional method of fishing. Fishermen make a hole in lake or sea ice with a long knife or pole. They lower a hooked line into the cold water. Some Inuit also fish with nets.

## Arctic dishes

Traditional meals include caribou stew and *mattaaq*. *Mattaaq* is whale skin with the blubber (fat) attached. It is very chewy, with a nutty taste. In the past, women skinned fish, carved meat, and prepared food. For this they used a special curved knife. It is called an *ulu*.

# Getting Around

There are few roads between towns in the **Arctic**. Some people drive all-terrain vehicles (ATVs) over rough ground. These have big, wide tires. The tires are good for traveling over rough ground. People prefer to use snowmobiles for driving on ice and snow.

◀ Snowmobiles are powered along on skis.

## Traditional travel

Before snowmobiles were invented, many Arctic people used **husky** dogs. The husky dogs worked in teams, pulling along sleds full of people and their belongings. Some Arctic hunters still use teams of huskies to pull sleds. Dog teams also take part in sporting competitions.

◀ Husky dogs are specially trained to pull sleds. They are willing and strong.

## ON WATER

The Inuit often hunt seals and other sea animals. It is traditional to hunt using a **kayak**. This is a narrow, pointed canoe. It has a light, wooden frame. The frame is covered with sealskin. Today, Inuit people and others also enjoy paddling kayaks for fun and as a sport.

# Inuit Beliefs

Inuit children were brought up to believe in spirits. They were told many **myths**. These historical stories and other **legends** keep the spirit tradition alive. Today, many Inuit have become Christians. There are churches in towns and villages.

▸ This is an Anglican (Christian) church in Nunavut. Families attend church services on Sundays.

## The spirit world

In the past, the Inuit believed that all people and animals had souls (spirits). Their souls lived on after death. The sun, moon, wind, and other natural things also had spirits. They were all controlled by a great life force called *Sila*. Special people in each Inuit **community** could make contact with the spirit world. These people were called **shamans**.

◀ This is a carving of the goddess Sedna. Her fingers have turned into seals and whales.

## THE SEA GODDESS

Inuit myths tell of a goddess who lives at the bottom of the sea. She is named Sedna. She was once a human girl, but is now a spirit. She is the ruler of seals, whales, and all the other sea animals. When she is angry, Sedna makes storms. The storms stop hunters from catching any of Sedna's sea creatures.

# Fun and Games

Many traditional outdoor games are based on hunting. Fathers teach their boys to hit a target with a **harpoon**. A harpoon is a spear attached to a long cord. Another game is to sling a **bola**. A bola has stone weights attached to the end of cords.

Today, children like ice skating, ice hockey, and sledding. People also like to race snowmobiles and dog teams.

▲ Blanket tossing is a traditional game.
The blanket is made of sealskin.

## Inside

A popular indoor game is called *ayagak*. A piece of bone is drilled with holes and attached to a string. At the other end of the string is a pin. Players throw up the bone and try to catch it on the pin.

▸ A popular Inuit sport is one foot high kick.

## ARCTIC WINTER GAMES

The **Arctic** Winter Games are held every two years. They take place in a different area in the Arctic region each time. In addition to skiing and snowboarding, there are many Inuit games. One is the kneel jump competition. A kneeling athlete jumps forward as far as possible.

# Arts and Crafts

The Inuit have a long tradition of carving. They carve from many different materials found in the **Arctic**. For centuries they made tools, containers, and toys. They carved them out of bone from dead animals, such as **caribou**. Caribou **antlers** were often carved. They also used **ivory** from walrus or **narwhal** tusks. A narwhal is a small whale. Today, the Inuit also make small figurines and charms to wear around the neck.

◀ This craftsman is carving a figure from soft stone.

## TOURIST ATTRACTION

Today, Inuit craftworkers are well known for their use of local stones, such as serpentine and soapstone. In larger villages, they carve and sell stone figurines. These are very popular with tourists visiting the Arctic.

▲ The Inuit also like to draw
pictures from Inuit myths.

## Drawings and prints

Today, artists celebrate their Inuit traditions and
**culture**. They draw, paint, and print traditional
Arctic subjects. These include polar animals such as
bears, caribou, seals, fish, and birds. Artists also like
to draw Inuit **myths**, such as the story of Sedna
(see page 19).

# Stories and Music

During winter, storytelling, singing, and dancing are important in Inuit **communities**. The most popular stories are **legends**. They are about magic, spirits, and the world. One favorite tale is about a **shaman**.

One day long ago, he chopped down a tree for firewood. But the wood chips flew into a lake and turned into fish. The shaman continued chopping, but the same thing happened again. That is why there are plenty of fish in the Inuit lands, but no trees.

▸ Inuit singers face each other in a singing contest.

## Drum dancing

Inuit often dance to the beat of drums. The drums are made of **caribou** skin. The skin is stretched over a round frame made of **antler**. Singers join in with the music. Today, drum dancing is performed on special occasions, such as birth, marriage, or the changing seasons.

▶ The musician holds the drum by its handle. He strikes the frame with a thick drumstick.

## SPRING FESTIVAL

The Toonik Tyme is a spring festival. It takes place each April in Iqaluit, the capital of Nunavut. The festival lasts for a week. There are games and competitions. These include dogsled and snowmobile racing, snow-house building, and ice sculpture. There are also community feasts.

# Make an inukshuk

Inuit hunters and travelers often put up a human-shaped column of stones. This is called an *inukshuk*. "*Inukshuk*" means "like a person." Hunters used them to frighten **caribou**. They were also built to warn travelers of danger, such as a cliff. Some Inuit used *inukshuks* to mark a good hunting spot, or to mark a place where the family had stored food supplies. Today, *inukshuks* are used to mark trails.

▶ This *inukshuk* stands on Baffin Island, in Nunavut.

**To make an *inukshuk*, you will need:**
air-hardening clay, white poster
paint, clay varnish, a modeling tool,
and a brush.

**1.** First, make the feet. Mold two lumps
of clay into rough cubes. Make four
more clay cubes for the legs. Each pair should be
slightly smaller than the feet.

**2.** For the body, flatten and model a lump of clay into
a sturdy slab. Make two more, slightly shorter slabs.
Make a very long slab for the arms.

**3.** Mold the neck and head using
two lumps of clay. Put the column
together while the clay is still moist.
Scratch and moisten the joining
surfaces. Gently press them together.
Smooth over the joins.

**4.** When your *inukshuk* is dry,
paint it white. Leave the paint to
dry, then varnish it. Ask an adult
to help.

# Inuit History

The first people to set foot in North America were hunters from Asia. This happened about 20,000 years ago. The hunters walked across frozen land. This land is now the seabed of the Bering Strait. The Bering Strait is a narrow passage of sea. It separates the country of Russia, in Asia, from the U.S. state of Alaska (see map on page 4).

▲ Europeans arrive in the Arctic.
They trade with the Inuit.

## Hunting and trading

Over 1,000 years ago, the Thule people came to the **Arctic**. They built **kayaks** and hunted whales. They were **ancestors** of the Inuit. Around 500 years ago, the first European whalers and fishermen reached the Arctic. Much later, Europeans and Americans began trading with the Inuit.

It was only recently that the Inuit were given their own **territory**—the Nunavut.

▸ Inuit shoppers use snowmobiles to visit their nearest store.

## THE FUR TRADE

The Arctic fur trade was very important to the Europeans and Americans. The Inuit traded fur in return for wood, iron, and firearms. But the newcomers also brought deadly diseases, such as **smallpox** and measles. Many Inuit died.

# Find Out for Yourself

## Books to read

Alexander, Bryan and Cherry. *Journey into the Arctic*. New York: Oxford, 2003.

Houston, James. *James Houston's Treasury of Inuit Legends*. Orlando, Fla.: Harcourt, 2006.

Kalman, Bobbie, and Rebecca Sjonger. *Life in the Far North*. New York: Crabtree, 2003.

Mack, Lorrie. *Arctic and Antarctic*. New York: Dorling Kindersley, 2006.

Williams, Suzanne M. *The Inuit*. New York: Franklin Watts, 2003.

## Websites

**www.athropolis.com/library-alpha.htm**
An A–Z library of interesting information about life in the Arctic.

**www.awg.ca**
The official site of the Arctic Winter Games.

**www.i4at.org/lib2/igloo.htm**
A simple page on how to make an igloo—if you have enough snow to try it!

**www.mnh.si.edu/arctic/html/wildlife.html**
A good presentation of Arctic wildlife by the Arctic Studies Center, Alaska.

**Disclaimer**
All the Internet addresses (URLs) given in this book were valid at the time of going to press. However, due to the dynamic nature of the Internet, some addresses may have changed, or sites may have ceased to exist since publication. While the author and publishers regret any inconvenience this may cause readers, no responsibility for any such changes can be accepted by either the author or the publishers. It is recommended that adults supervise children on the Internet.

# Glossary

**ancestor** parent, grandparent, great-grandparent, and any past relative of a particular family

**antler** branched horns on the head of caribou and other deer

**Arctic** cold region at the top of the world, near the North Pole

**bola** number of stones connected by strong cord that can be swung around and hurled at a target

**caribou** large deer similar to the reindeer

**community** group of people who live in the same place

**culture** customs and way of life of a particular group of people

**dialect** regional variation of a language

**driftwood** pieces of wood that are found washed up on shore

**harpoon** sharp weapon, such as a spear, that is attached to a long cord and thrown. It is often used for hunting whales.

**husky** arctic breed of dog trained to pull sleds

**ivory** hard material from the tusks of the walrus or narwahl used for carving

**kayak** light, pointed, covered canoe

**legend** traditional story about the past that may or may not be true

**moss** small, short plant that does not flower and can grow on rock

**myth** traditional story, often of heroes, gods, and spirits

**narwhal** small whale. Male narwhals have a single, long tusk.

**settlement** place where people have settled and built their homes

**shaman** person who is believed to be able to make contact with the world of spirits

**shrub** bushy plant

**smallpox** life-threatening disease that causes pockmarks on the skin

**territory** area of land that is also an official region (such as a province of Canada)

**tundra** flat, treeless region where the ground is very cold

# Index